TIME LOG BOOK

FOR KAYAK AND CANOE ATHLETES

THIS BOOK BELONGS TO:

....

....

START DATE: ....

END DATE: ....

Time Trials, Personal Bests and Races

Date	Course	Distance	Time

Time Trials, Personal Bests and Races

Date	Course	Distance	Time

Time Trials, Personal Bests and Races

Date	Course	Distance	Time

Time Trials, Personal Bests and Races

Date	Course	Distance	Time

Date		Course			Time		☆PB
Lap Times	1		2		3	4	5
	6		7		8	9	10
Notes:							☹ ☹ 😐 🙂 😍

Date		Course			Time		☆PB
Lap Times	1		2		3	4	5
	6		7		8	9	10
Notes:							☹ ☹ 😐 🙂 😍

Date		Course			Time		☆PB
Lap Times	1		2		3	4	5
	6		7		8	9	10
Notes:							☹ ☹ 😐 🙂 😍

Date		Course			Time		☆PB
Lap Times	1		2		3	4	5
	6		7		8	9	10
Notes:							☹ ☹ 😐 🙂 😍

Date		Course			Time		☆ PB
Lap Times	1	2		3	4	5	
	6	7		8	9	10	
Notes:							

😕 😟 😐 🙂 😍

Date		Course			Time		☆ PB
Lap Times	1	2		3	4	5	
	6	7		8	9	10	
Notes:							

😕 😟 😐 🙂 😍

Date		Course			Time		☆ PB
Lap Times	1	2		3	4	5	
	6	7		8	9	10	
Notes:							

😕 😟 😐 🙂 😍

Date		Course			Time		☆ PB
Lap Times	1	2		3	4	5	
	6	7		8	9	10	
Notes:							

😕 😟 😐 🙂 😍

Date		Course			Time		☆PB

Lap Times	1	2	3	4	5
	6	7	8	9	10

Notes:

☹ 🙁 😐 🙂 😍

Date		Course			Time		☆PB

Lap Times	1	2	3	4	5
	6	7	8	9	10

Notes:

☹ 🙁 😐 🙂 😍

Date		Course			Time		☆PB

Lap Times	1	2	3	4	5
	6	7	8	9	10

Notes:

☹ 🙁 😐 🙂 😍

Date		Course			Time		☆PB

Lap Times	1	2	3	4	5
	6	7	8	9	10

Notes:

☹ 🙁 😐 🙂 😍

Date		Course			Time		☆
Lap Times	1	2		3	4	5	
	6	7		8	9	10	

Notes:

☹ ☹ 😐 ☺ 😍

Date		Course			Time		☆
Lap Times	1	2		3	4	5	
	6	7		8	9	10	

Notes:

☹ ☹ 😐 ☺ 😍

Date		Course			Time		☆
Lap Times	1	2		3	4	5	
	6	7		8	9	10	

Notes:

☹ ☹ 😐 ☺ 😍

Date		Course			Time		☆
Lap Times	1	2		3	4	5	
	6	7		8	9	10	

Notes:

☹ ☹ 😐 ☺ 😍

Date		Course			Time		☆
Lap Times	1	2		3	4		5
	6	7		8	9		10
Notes:							
					☹ ☹ 😐 ☺ 😍		

Date		Course			Time		☆
Lap Times	1	2		3	4		5
	6	7		8	9		10
Notes:							
					☹ ☹ 😐 ☺ 😍		

Date		Course			Time		☆
Lap Times	1	2		3	4		5
	6	7		8	9		10
Notes:							
					☹ ☹ 😐 ☺ 😍		

Date		Course			Time		☆
Lap Times	1	2		3	4		5
	6	7		8	9		10
Notes:							
					☹ ☹ 😐 ☺ 😍		

Date		Course			Time		☆
Lap Times	1		2	3	4		5
	6		7	8	9		10
Notes:							

☹ 😕 😐 🙂 😍

Date		Course			Time		☆
Lap Times	1		2	3	4		5
	6		7	8	9		10
Notes:							

☹ 😕 😐 🙂 😍

Date		Course			Time		☆
Lap Times	1		2	3	4		5
	6		7	8	9		10
Notes:							

☹ 😕 😐 🙂 😍

Date		Course			Time		☆
Lap Times	1		2	3	4		5
	6		7	8	9		10
Notes:							

☹ 😕 😐 🙂 😍

Date		Course		Time		☆PB

Lap Times

1	2	3	4	5
6	7	8	9	10

Notes:

☹ ☹ 😐 🙂 😍

Date		Course		Time		☆PB

Lap Times

1	2	3	4	5
6	7	8	9	10

Notes:

☹ ☹ 😐 🙂 😍

Date		Course		Time		☆PB

Lap Times

1	2	3	4	5
6	7	8	9	10

Notes:

☹ ☹ 😐 🙂 😍

Date		Course		Time		☆PB

Lap Times

1	2	3	4	5
6	7	8	9	10

Notes:

☹ ☹ 😐 🙂 😍

Date		Course			Time		☆

Lap Times	1	2	3	4	5
	6	7	8	9	10

Notes:

☹ ☹ 😐 🙂 😍

Date		Course			Time		☆

Lap Times	1	2	3	4	5
	6	7	8	9	10

Notes:

☹ ☹ 😐 🙂 😍

Date		Course			Time		☆

Lap Times	1	2	3	4	5
	6	7	8	9	10

Notes:

☹ ☹ 😐 🙂 😍

Date		Course			Time		☆

Lap Times	1	2	3	4	5
	6	7	8	9	10

Notes:

☹ ☹ 😐 🙂 😍

Date		Course			Time		☆PB

Lap Times

1	2	3	4	5
6	7	8	9	10

Notes:

☹ ☹ 😐 ☺ 😍

Date		Course			Time		☆PB

Lap Times

1	2	3	4	5
6	7	8	9	10

Notes:

☹ ☹ 😐 ☺ 😍

Date		Course			Time		☆PB

Lap Times

1	2	3	4	5
6	7	8	9	10

Notes:

☹ ☹ 😐 ☺ 😍

Date		Course			Time		☆PB

Lap Times

1	2	3	4	5
6	7	8	9	10

Notes:

☹ ☹ 😐 ☺ 😍

Date		Course			Time		☆
Lap Times	1	2		3	4	5	
	6	7		8	9	10	
Notes:							

☹ 😕 😐 🙂 😍

Date		Course			Time		☆
Lap Times	1	2		3	4	5	
	6	7		8	9	10	
Notes:							

☹ 😕 😐 🙂 😍

Date		Course			Time		☆
Lap Times	1	2		3	4	5	
	6	7		8	9	10	
Notes:							

☹ 😕 😐 🙂 😍

Date		Course			Time		☆
Lap Times	1	2		3	4	5	
	6	7		8	9	10	
Notes:							

☹ 😕 😐 🙂 😍

Date		Course			Time		☆ PB
Lap Times	1	2	3	4		5	
	6	7	8	9		10	

Notes:

☹ ☹ 😐 🙂 😍

Date		Course			Time		☆ PB
Lap Times	1	2	3	4		5	
	6	7	8	9		10	

Notes:

☹ ☹ 😐 🙂 😍

Date		Course			Time		☆ PB
Lap Times	1	2	3	4		5	
	6	7	8	9		10	

Notes:

☹ ☹ 😐 🙂 😍

Date		Course			Time		☆ PB
Lap Times	1	2	3	4		5	
	6	7	8	9		10	

Notes:

☹ ☹ 😐 🙂 😍

Date		Course			Time		☆PB

Lap Times	1	2	3	4	5
	6	7	8	9	10

Notes:

😖 😟 😐 🙂 😍

Date		Course			Time		☆PB

Lap Times	1	2	3	4	5
	6	7	8	9	10

Notes:

😖 😟 😐 🙂 😍

Date		Course			Time		☆PB

Lap Times	1	2	3	4	5
	6	7	8	9	10

Notes:

😖 😟 😐 🙂 😍

Date		Course			Time		☆PB

Lap Times	1	2	3	4	5
	6	7	8	9	10

Notes:

Date		Course			Time		☆

Lap Times	1	2	3	4	5
	6	7	8	9	10

Notes:

🙁 🙁 😐 🙂 😍

Date		Course			Time		☆

Lap Times	1	2	3	4	5
	6	7	8	9	10

Notes:

🙁 🙁 😐 🙂 😍

Date		Course			Time		☆

Lap Times	1	2	3	4	5
	6	7	8	9	10

Notes:

🙁 🙁 😐 🙂 😍

Date		Course			Time		☆

Lap Times	1	2	3	4	5
	6	7	8	9	10

Notes:

🙁 🙁 😐 🙂 😍

Date		Course			Time		☆PB
Lap Times	1	2		3	4		5
	6	7		8	9		10
Notes:							☹ ☹ 😐 🙂 😍

Date		Course			Time		☆PB
Lap Times	1	2		3	4		5
	6	7		8	9		10
Notes:							☹ ☹ 😐 🙂 😍

Date		Course			Time		☆PB
Lap Times	1	2		3	4		5
	6	7		8	9		10
Notes:							☹ ☹ 😐 🙂 😍

Date		Course			Time		☆PB
Lap Times	1	2		3	4		5
	6	7		8	9		10
Notes:							☹ ☹ 😐 🙂 😍

Date		Course		Time		☆ PB

Lap Times	1	2	3	4	5
	6	7	8	9	10

Notes:

😞 😕 😐 🙂 😍

Date		Course		Time		☆ PB

Lap Times	1	2	3	4	5
	6	7	8	9	10

Notes:

😞 😕 😐 🙂 😍

Date		Course		Time		☆ PB

Lap Times	1	2	3	4	5
	6	7	8	9	10

Notes:

😞 😕 😐 🙂 😍

Date		Course		Time		☆ PB

Lap Times	1	2	3	4	5
	6	7	8	9	10

Notes:

Date		Course			Time		☆ PB
Lap Times	1	2		3	4		5
	6	7		8	9		10

Notes:

☹ 🙁 😐 🙂 😍

Date		Course			Time		☆ PB
Lap Times	1	2		3	4		5
	6	7		8	9		10

Notes:

☹ 🙁 😐 🙂 😍

Date		Course			Time		☆ PB
Lap Times	1	2		3	4		5
	6	7		8	9		10

Notes:

☹ 🙁 😐 🙂 😍

Date		Course			Time		☆ PB
Lap Times	1	2		3	4		5
	6	7		8	9		10

Notes:

☹ 🙁 😐 🙂 😍

Date		Course			Time		☆

Lap Times	1	2	3	4	5
	6	7	8	9	10

Notes:

😫 😟 😐 🙂 😍

Date		Course			Time		☆

Lap Times	1	2	3	4	5
	6	7	8	9	10

Notes:

😫 😟 😐 🙂 😍

Date		Course			Time		☆

Lap Times	1	2	3	4	5
	6	7	8	9	10

Notes:

😫 😟 😐 🙂 😍

Date		Course			Time		☆

Lap Times	1	2	3	4	5
	6	7	8	9	10

Notes:

😫 😟 😐 🙂 😍

Date		Course		Time		☆
Lap Times	1	2	3	4	5	
	6	7	8	9	10	
Notes:						☹ 😕 😐 🙂 😍

Date		Course		Time		☆
Lap Times	1	2	3	4	5	
	6	7	8	9	10	
Notes:						☹ 😕 😐 🙂 😍

Date		Course		Time		☆
Lap Times	1	2	3	4	5	
	6	7	8	9	10	
Notes:						☹ 😕 😐 🙂 😍

Date		Course		Time		☆
Lap Times	1	2	3	4	5	
	6	7	8	9	10	
Notes:						☹ 😕 😐 🙂 😍

Date		Course			Time		☆ PB
Lap Times	1	2		3	4		5
	6	7		8	9		10
Notes:							
							☹ ☹ 😐 🙂 😍

Date		Course			Time		☆ PB
Lap Times	1	2		3	4		5
	6	7		8	9		10
Notes:							
							☹ ☹ 😐 🙂 😍

Date		Course			Time		☆ PB
Lap Times	1	2		3	4		5
	6	7		8	9		10
Notes:							
							☹ ☹ 😐 🙂 😍

Date		Course			Time		☆ PB
Lap Times	1	2		3	4		5
	6	7		8	9		10
Notes:							
							☹ ☹ 😐 🙂 😍

Date		Course			Time		☆

Lap Times	1	2	3	4	5
	6	7	8	9	10

Notes:

😟 😕 😐 🙂 😍

Date		Course			Time		☆

Lap Times	1	2	3	4	5
	6	7	8	9	10

Notes:

😟 😕 😐 🙂 😍

Date		Course			Time		☆

Lap Times	1	2	3	4	5
	6	7	8	9	10

Notes:

😟 😕 😐 🙂 😍

Date		Course			Time		☆

Lap Times	1	2	3	4	5
	6	7	8	9	10

Notes:

😟 😕 😐 🙂 😍

Date		Course		Time		☆

Lap Times	1	2	3	4	5
	6	7	8	9	10

Notes:

Date		Course		Time		☆

Lap Times	1	2	3	4	5
	6	7	8	9	10

Notes:

Date		Course		Time		☆

Lap Times	1	2	3	4	5
	6	7	8	9	10

Notes:

Date		Course		Time		☆

Lap Times	1	2	3	4	5
	6	7	8	9	10

Notes:

Date		Course			Time		☆
Lap Times	1	2	3	4	5		
	6	7	8	9	10		

Notes:

☹ ☹ ☺ ☺ 😍

Date		Course			Time		☆
Lap Times	1	2	3	4	5		
	6	7	8	9	10		

Notes:

☹ ☹ ☺ ☺ 😍

Date		Course			Time		☆
Lap Times	1	2	3	4	5		
	6	7	8	9	10		

Notes:

☹ ☹ ☺ ☺ 😍

Date		Course			Time		☆
Lap Times	1	2	3	4	5		
	6	7	8	9	10		

Notes:

☹ ☹ ☺ ☺ 😍

Date		Course			Time		☆
Lap Times	1	2		3	4		5
	6	7		8	9		10
Notes:							☹ ☹ 😐 ☺ 😍

Date		Course			Time		☆
Lap Times	1	2		3	4		5
	6	7		8	9		10
Notes:							☹ ☹ 😐 ☺ 😍

Date		Course			Time		☆
Lap Times	1	2		3	4		5
	6	7		8	9		10
Notes:							☹ ☹ 😐 ☺ 😍

Date		Course			Time		☆
Lap Times	1	2		3	4		5
	6	7		8	9		10
Notes:							☹ ☹ 😐 ☺ 😍

Date		Course		Time		

Lap Times	1	2	3	4	5
	6	7	8	9	10

Notes:

Date		Course		Time		

Lap Times	1	2	3	4	5
	6	7	8	9	10

Notes:

Date		Course		Time		

Lap Times	1	2	3	4	5
	6	7	8	9	10

Notes:

Date		Course		Time		

Lap Times	1	2	3	4	5
	6	7	8	9	10

Notes:

Date		Course			Time		☆
Lap Times	1	2		3	4	5	
	6	7		8	9	10	
Notes:							☹ ☹ 😐 🙂 😍

Date		Course			Time		☆
Lap Times	1	2		3	4	5	
	6	7		8	9	10	
Notes:							☹ ☹ 😐 🙂 😍

Date		Course			Time		☆
Lap Times	1	2		3	4	5	
	6	7		8	9	10	
Notes:							☹ ☹ 😐 🙂 😍

Date		Course			Time		☆
Lap Times	1	2		3	4	5	
	6	7		8	9	10	
Notes:							☹ ☹ 😐 🙂 😍

Date		Course		Time		☆PB

Lap Times

1	2	3	4	5
6	7	8	9	10

Notes:

☹ ☹ 😐 🙂 😍

Date		Course		Time		☆PB

Lap Times

1	2	3	4	5
6	7	8	9	10

Notes:

☹ ☹ 😐 🙂 😍

Date		Course		Time		☆PB

Lap Times

1	2	3	4	5
6	7	8	9	10

Notes:

☹ ☹ 😐 🙂 😍

Date		Course		Time		☆PB

Lap Times

1	2	3	4	5
6	7	8	9	10

Notes:

☹ ☹ 😐 🙂 😍

Date		Course			Time		☆PB

Lap Times	1	2	3	4	5
	6	7	8	9	10

Notes:

☹ ☹ 😐 🙂 😍

Date		Course			Time		☆PB

Lap Times	1	2	3	4	5
	6	7	8	9	10

Notes:

☹ ☹ 😐 🙂 😍

Date		Course			Time		☆PB

Lap Times	1	2	3	4	5
	6	7	8	9	10

Notes:

☹ ☹ 😐 🙂 😍

Date		Course			Time		☆PB

Lap Times	1	2	3	4	5
	6	7	8	9	10

Notes:

☹ ☹ 😐 🙂 😍

Date		Course		Time		☆ PB

Lap Times

1	2	3	4	5
6	7	8	9	10

Notes:

☹ 😕 😐 🙂 😍

Date		Course		Time		☆ PB

Lap Times

1	2	3	4	5
6	7	8	9	10

Notes:

☹ 😕 😐 🙂 😍

Date		Course		Time		☆ PB

Lap Times

1	2	3	4	5
6	7	8	9	10

Notes:

☹ 😕 😐 🙂 😍

Date		Course		Time		☆ PB

Lap Times

1	2	3	4	5
6	7	8	9	10

Notes:

☹ 😕 😐 🙂 😍

Date		Course			Time		☆PB

Lap Times	1	2	3	4	5
	6	7	8	9	10

Notes:

🙁 ☹ 😐 🙂 😍

Date		Course			Time		☆PB

Lap Times	1	2	3	4	5
	6	7	8	9	10

Notes:

🙁 ☹ 😐 🙂 😍

Date		Course			Time		☆PB

Lap Times	1	2	3	4	5
	6	7	8	9	10

Notes:

🙁 ☹ 😐 🙂 😍

Date		Course			Time		☆PB

Lap Times	1	2	3	4	5
	6	7	8	9	10

Notes:

🙁 ☹ 😐 🙂 😍

Date		Course			Time		☆PB
Lap Times	1	2	3		4	5	
	6	7	8		9	10	

Notes:

😞 😕 😐 🙂 😍

Date		Course			Time		☆PB
Lap Times	1	2	3		4	5	
	6	7	8		9	10	

Notes:

😞 😕 😐 🙂 😍

Date		Course			Time		☆PB
Lap Times	1	2	3		4	5	
	6	7	8		9	10	

Notes:

😞 😕 😐 🙂 😍

Date		Course			Time		☆PB
Lap Times	1	2	3		4	5	
	6	7	8		9	10	

Notes:

😞 😕 😐 🙂 😍

Date		Course			Time		☆

Lap Times	1	2	3	4	5
	6	7	8	9	10

Notes:

☹ ☹ 😐 ☺ 😍

Date		Course			Time		☆

Lap Times	1	2	3	4	5
	6	7	8	9	10

Notes:

☹ ☹ 😐 ☺ 😍

Date		Course			Time		☆

Lap Times	1	2	3	4	5
	6	7	8	9	10

Notes:

☹ ☹ 😐 ☺ 😍

Date		Course			Time		☆

Lap Times	1	2	3	4	5
	6	7	8	9	10

Notes:

☹ ☹ 😐 ☺ 😍

Date		Course			Time		☆
Lap Times	1	2	3	4	5		
	6	7	8	9	10		
Notes:							

☹ ☹ 😐 🙂 😍

Date		Course			Time		☆
Lap Times	1	2	3	4	5		
	6	7	8	9	10		
Notes:							

☹ ☹ 😐 🙂 😍

Date		Course			Time		☆
Lap Times	1	2	3	4	5		
	6	7	8	9	10		
Notes:							

☹ ☹ 😐 🙂 😍

Date		Course			Time		☆
Lap Times	1	2	3	4	5		
	6	7	8	9	10		
Notes:							

☹ ☹ 😐 🙂 😍

Date		Course		Time		☆ PB

Lap Times	1	2	3	4	5
	6	7	8	9	10

Notes:

☹ ☹ 😐 🙂 😍

Date		Course		Time		☆ PB

Lap Times	1	2	3	4	5
	6	7	8	9	10

Notes:

☹ ☹ 😐 🙂 😍

Date		Course		Time		☆ PB

Lap Times	1	2	3	4	5
	6	7	8	9	10

Notes:

☹ ☹ 😐 🙂 😍

Date		Course		Time		☆ PB

Lap Times	1	2	3	4	5
	6	7	8	9	10

Notes:

☹ ☹ 😐 🙂 😍

Date		Course			Time		☆ PB

Lap Times	1	2	3	4	5
	6	7	8	9	10

Notes:

☹ 🙁 😐 🙂 😍

Date		Course			Time		☆ PB

Lap Times	1	2	3	4	5
	6	7	8	9	10

Notes:

☹ 🙁 😐 🙂 😍

Date		Course			Time		☆ PB

Lap Times	1	2	3	4	5
	6	7	8	9	10

Notes:

☹ 🙁 😐 🙂 😍

Date		Course			Time		☆ PB

Lap Times	1	2	3	4	5
	6	7	8	9	10

Notes:

☹ 🙁 😐 🙂 😍

Date		Course		Time		☆

Lap Times	1	2	3	4	5
	6	7	8	9	10

Notes:

☹ ☹ 😐 🙂 😍

Date		Course		Time		☆

Lap Times	1	2	3	4	5
	6	7	8	9	10

Notes:

☹ ☹ 😐 🙂 😍

Date		Course		Time		☆

Lap Times	1	2	3	4	5
	6	7	8	9	10

Notes:

☹ ☹ 😐 🙂 😍

Date		Course		Time		☆

Lap Times	1	2	3	4	5
	6	7	8	9	10

Notes:

☹ ☹ 😐 🙂 😍

Date		Course			Time		☆

Lap Times

1	2	3	4	5
6	7	8	9	10

Notes:

Date		Course			Time		☆

Lap Times

1	2	3	4	5
6	7	8	9	10

Notes:

Date		Course			Time		☆

Lap Times

1	2	3	4	5
6	7	8	9	10

Notes:

Date		Course			Time		☆

Lap Times

1	2	3	4	5
6	7	8	9	10

Notes:

Date		Course			Time		☆PB

Lap Times	1	2	3	4	5
	6	7	8	9	10

Notes:

☹ ☹ 😐 🙂 😎

Date		Course			Time		☆PB

Lap Times	1	2	3	4	5
	6	7	8	9	10

Notes:

☹ ☹ 😐 🙂 😎

Date		Course			Time		☆PB

Lap Times	1	2	3	4	5
	6	7	8	9	10

Notes:

☹ ☹ 😐 🙂 😎

Date		Course			Time		☆PB

Lap Times	1	2	3	4	5
	6	7	8	9	10

Notes:

☹ ☹ 😐 🙂 😎

Date		Course			Time		☆PB
Lap Times	1	2	3	4		5	
	6	7	8	9		10	
Notes:							☹ 😦 😐 🙂 😍

Date		Course			Time		☆PB
Lap Times	1	2	3	4		5	
	6	7	8	9		10	
Notes:							☹ 😦 😐 🙂 😍

Date		Course			Time		☆PB
Lap Times	1	2	3	4		5	
	6	7	8	9		10	
Notes:							☹ 😦 😐 🙂 😍

Date		Course			Time		☆PB
Lap Times	1	2	3	4		5	
	6	7	8	9		10	
Notes:							☹ 😦 😐 🙂 😍

Date		Course			Time		☆PB
Lap Times	1	2	3	4		5	
	6	7	8	9		10	

Notes:

☹ 🙁 😐 🙂 😍

Date		Course			Time		☆PB
Lap Times	1	2	3	4		5	
	6	7	8	9		10	

Notes:

☹ 🙁 😐 🙂 😍

Date		Course			Time		☆PB
Lap Times	1	2	3	4		5	
	6	7	8	9		10	

Notes:

☹ 🙁 😐 🙂 😍

Date		Course			Time		☆PB
Lap Times	1	2	3	4		5	
	6	7	8	9		10	

Notes:

☹ 🙁 😐 🙂 😍

Date		Course			Time		☆

Lap Times	1	2	3	4	5
	6	7	8	9	10

Notes:

☹ 😧 😐 🙂 😍

Date		Course			Time		☆

Lap Times	1	2	3	4	5
	6	7	8	9	10

Notes:

☹ 😧 😐 🙂 😍

Date		Course			Time		☆

Lap Times	1	2	3	4	5
	6	7	8	9	10

Notes:

☹ 😧 😐 🙂 😍

Date		Course			Time		☆

Lap Times	1	2	3	4	5
	6	7	8	9	10

Notes:

☹ 😧 😐 🙂 😍

Date		Course			Time		☆PB

Lap Times	1	2	3	4	5
	6	7	8	9	10

Notes:

☹ 🙁 😐 🙂 😍

Date		Course			Time		☆PB

Lap Times	1	2	3	4	5
	6	7	8	9	10

Notes:

☹ 🙁 😐 🙂 😍

Date		Course			Time		☆PB

Lap Times	1	2	3	4	5
	6	7	8	9	10

Notes:

☹ 🙁 😐 🙂 😍

Date		Course			Time		☆PB

Lap Times	1	2	3	4	5
	6	7	8	9	10

Notes:

☹ 🙁 😐 🙂 😍

Date		Course			Time		☆PB
Lap Times	1	2	3	4		5	
	6	7	8	9		10	
Notes:							☹ 😦 😐 🙂 😍

Date		Course			Time		☆PB
Lap Times	1	2	3	4		5	
	6	7	8	9		10	
Notes:							☹ 😦 😐 🙂 😍

Date		Course			Time		☆PB
Lap Times	1	2	3	4		5	
	6	7	8	9		10	
Notes:							☹ 😦 😐 🙂 😍

Date		Course			Time		☆PB
Lap Times	1	2	3	4		5	
	6	7	8	9		10	
Notes:							☹ 😦 😐 🙂 😍

Progress Plotter

Course: ....

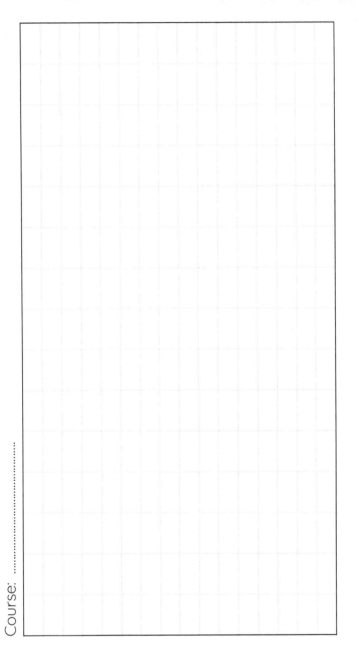

Time

Date

Progress Plotter

Course: ....

Time

Date

Progress Plotter

Course: ....

Time

Date

Progress Plotter

Course: ....

Time

Date

Progress Plotter

Course: ....

Time

Date

Progress Plotter

Course: ....

Time

Date

Progress Plotter

Course: ....

Time

Date

Progress Plotter

Course: ....

Time

Date

Progress Plotter

Course: ....

Time

Date

Progress Plotter

Course: ....

Time

Date

Progress Plotter

Course: ....

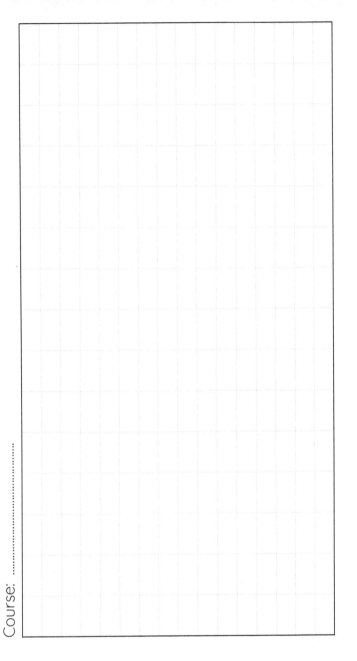

Time

Date

Progress Plotter

Course: ....

Time

Date

Made in United States
Troutdale, OR
06/16/2024

20608465R00056